THEN & NOW

MATHEWS COUNTY

James Nagel

December 2011

THEN & NOW

MATHEWS COUNTY

Janice C. Vogel

This book is dedicated to my children, Sam and Maria Spadaccini, for whom I returned to Mathews so they would grow up never far from the water or a friendly face.

Library of Congress Control Number: 2011929816

Published by Arcadia Publishing
Charleston, South Carolina

Printed in the United States of America

For all general information, please contact Arcadia Publishing:
Telephone 843-853-2070
Fax 843-853-0044
E-mail sales@arcadiapublishing.com
For customer service and orders:
Toll-Free 1-888-313-2665

Visit us on the Internet at www.arcadiapublishing.com

On the Front Cover: The northwest view of Main Street in the mid-20th century is virtually unchanged today. (Then image courtesy of Tidewater Newspapers, Inc.; now image courtesy of the author.)

On the Back Cover: A little further up Main Street, the northeast view looks very different today and now includes the Food Lion shopping center. (Courtesy of Tidewater Newspapers, Inc.)

CONTENTS

ACKNOWLEDGMENTS

Quite simply, this book would not exist without the generosity of Elsa Cooke Verbyla and Charlie Koenig, publisher and editor, respectively, of the *Gazette-Journal*. Thank you for allowing me unlimited access to the treasure trove of history and photographs in the *Gazette-Journal*'s library in Gloucester.

Unless otherwise noted, all of the then photographs are from the *Mathews Journal* or the *Gazette-Journal*, published by Tidewater Newspapers, Inc. All now photographs are courtesy of the author.

In addition to the *Gazette-Journal*'s library and archives, there were three essential references for the compilation of this book: *History and Progress, Mathews County, Virginia* and *Mathews County Panorama*, both by the Mathews County Historical Society; and Images of America: *Mathews County* by Sara E. Lewis. If you're even remotely interested in the history of Mathews, add these books to your collection.

The Mathews Memorial Library's Chesapeake Room was another invaluable source of information. Headlines from the *Mathews Journal* are available on a searchable database, and early editions of the *Mathews Journal* and *Gazette-Journal* are viewable on microfilm. They have an extensive collection of local history books and many other resources, including the Herman Hollerith Archives.

Thanks also to Ray Hunley, commissioner of the revenue, and his staff and Eugene Callis, clerk of the circuit court, and his staff for their help and patience with my inquiries.

Many individuals contributed to this project. Thanks to my classmate Johnny Pugh for sharing his photographs and knowledge about Sandbank, Bayside, and New Point. Thanks to my friend Jim Stepka, who loaned me the laptop that I carried back and forth to the *Gazette-Journal*'s offices and the library. A special thanks to Bud Ward for delivering food when I was too busy and tired to cook.

Thanks to my friends, including those on Facebook, who so willingly—and quickly—answered my questions about dates, places, and people and who supported and encouraged me throughout this yearlong ordeal.

Last but not least, I thank my parents, Sam and Mary Ann Vogel, who helped me with everything I had to neglect in order to complete this project.

INTRODUCTION

Mathews County is a secluded community well off the beaten path, located on the eastern tip of Tidewater's Middle Peninsula on the western shore of the Chesapeake Bay. The second smallest county in Virginia at 84 square miles, it boasts 214 miles of shoreline—more than any other county on the bay.

The rich and varied history of Mathews dates back to the 1600s, when English colonists settled the area already inhabited by the Chiskiake Indians. In 1776, Lord John Dunmore, the last colonial governor of Virginia, was driven from his encampment at Gwynn's Island during the Battle of Cricket Hill, ending British rule in Virginia. The county was formally established in 1791 from a portion of Gloucester known as Kingston Parish.

With its proximity to the water, Mathews was a major center for shipbuilding as far back as the Revolutionary War, producing nearly one third of the ships built in Virginia between 1790 and 1820. The county was also an official port of entry for the registration and enrollment of all US and foreign vessels from 1802 to 1844. Thomas Jefferson commissioned the New Point Lighthouse, the third-oldest lighthouse still standing on the Chesapeake Bay.

Historical structures, some dating back to Colonial times, abound in the area. The Court Green, which includes the former courthouse and debtor's jail, dates back to the late 18th century. Historical plantations include Woodstock, Providence, Auburn, Green Plains, and Hesse, all of which are privately owned and well preserved. A Methodist tabernacle, in the Registry of Historic Places, is one of the last remaining examples of outdoor pavilions used for religious purposes.

In addition to its history, Mathews is well known for its natural beauty, small-town charm, friendly people, and resistance to change. The county's geographic isolation helps shield it from the rapid development in neighboring areas. Surrounded by water on three sides and adorned with undeveloped beaches, Mathews County is a destination, not a thoroughfare or a crossroads community. Aside from the lights on the Gwynn's Island Bridge, the county has no traffic signals, a topic that has been discussed and debated since 1935.

Then & Now: *Mathews County* attempts to provide the reader with past and present glimpses of sites that have helped define Mathews. The county is one of the few places left that has not sacrificed its older homes, country stores, wharves, or other charms to development. However, many of these places are in a state of decay, so capturing them now before they succumb is increasingly important.

This book is not intended to be a comprehensive history of the county. The original vision included chapters devoted to churches, schools, historic homes, and wharves. Entire books can be written on these topics alone. However, it became evident as the book evolved that the vast majority of older photographs of high enough quality to be used were of the Mathews Court House area—especially given the constraints of time and space. The topics presented in this book, therefore, were very much dictated by the older photographs found. As a result, numerous noteworthy and historically important places had to be omitted.

The chapters on the Court House area are grouped by the era in which the then photographs were taken. Efforts were made to provide a balance of local lore with historical facts where possible. Oversights and omissions are wholly unintentional but inevitable. I welcome comments and feedback and hope you enjoy this first attempt at a photographic journey through some of the highlights of this gem of a county known as Mathews.

CHAPTER 1

MATHEWS COURT HOUSE IN THE EARLY 20TH CENTURY

Rural Mathews County's downtown commercial and government sector is known simultaneously as the Court House, the Village and, originally, Westville. The name Westville likely originated from some of the earliest settlers who came across the Chesapeake Bay from Eastville on the Eastern Shore of Virginia.

Originally thought to have been built by Richard Billups in approximately 1793, the Mathews courthouse was described in an 1835 edition of *Martin's Gazetteer* as "a very neat new Court House," suggesting a later date. Clues in its construction, including mature machine-cut nails, support the 1830s date. Today, the official court offices are located at the recently constructed Liberty Square on the site of the former Lee-Jackson School. The original courthouse is still used for public meetings.

Built in 1859 one block from the courthouse, Westville Christian is one of the oldest churches in Mathews Court House. The church was formed by members of Mathews Baptist Church and Emmaus Baptist Church who were influenced by the growing Disciples of Christ movement in Virginia led by Rev. Alexander Campbell. Campbell's father, Rev. Thomas Campbell, visited and taught in Mathews County. Westville's history includes an 1865 raid by Union forces that stole the communion chalice.

Hyco House, located across from
Hardee's at the intersection of Routes
198 and 14, was built by William
Smith Todd in 1837 on 47 acres.
Todd, who lived here with his wife,
Eliza Hudgins Todd, also owned
a 250-acre plantation nearby. The
house had several owners before
being purchased in 1918 by Mathews
physician Dr. J.W.D. Haynes. The
home stayed in his family until 1990.

This c. 1900 photograph shows Ashley White's Mathews Drug Store, which sat at the corner of Brickbat Road and Main Street. Dr. C.C. White, who also taught school in a two-room school nearby, had an office here. The 1921 fire destroyed this building, along with the Jarvis and Pugh Department Store, the post office, a blacksmith's shop, a garage, and a grocery. Today, this corner, home to Real Goods and Hudgins Pharmacy, looks very different.

This view of Main Street looking north shows one drastic change in the streetscape over time. Wooden structures were gradually replaced by brick buildings due to the very real threat of fire. There were two very destructive fires in the Court House during the early 20th century, in 1921 and 1926. Mathews Drug Store was rebuilt after the 1921 fire but later moved to the old Farmers and Fishermens Bank (Hudgins Pharmacy today), the columned building on the left above.

The September 11, 1912, unveiling of the Confederate monument on the court green was reported by the *Mathews Journal* as a day of oppressive heat and dusty roads, which was not especially welcome in the days of ankle-length dresses. The statue was erected by the Lane-Diggs Camp of the Confederate Veterans and the Captain Sally Thompkins Chapter of the United Daughters of the Confederacy. Col. Robert E. Lee Jr., son of the general, was the main speaker at the unveiling.

This 1918 image of Main Street at Maple Avenue shows, from left to right, a glimpse of the Sibley Brothers General Store, built in 1899; the Wyatt Wolffe department store; and the Bank of Mathews. This prime streetfront property was originally owned by Thomas James, who as far back as 1810 operated a business here. Sibley's General Store, now listed in the National Register of Historic Places, serves as the Mathews Visitor and Information Center. The Mathews Memorial Library occupies the remaining space.

This early image is of the rectory at Kingston Parish on Main Street. The earliest places of worship in the county were chapels, and one was located on the North River and another near Queens Creek. St. John's Church, constructed in 1898 and dismantled in 1954, was located on the property where Kingston's Parish House now stands. Slight modifications have been made to the rectory over the years.

This c. 1924 photograph taken from the intersection of Court and Church Streets shows, from left to right, the old Lee Miles General Store, the Jarvis and Pugh Building, Mathews County Marble and Concrete Company, and Richardson's Drug Store. Over the years, the Jarvis and Pugh Building has been home to the Golden Brooks Shop, doctors, and other professional offices. Today, this view includes two additional structures, one of which served as Rosie's Gift Shop, an extension of Richardson's Drug Store.

Businesses along Main Street in 1923 included a tailor, the Mathews Garage, and Sibley's General Store, which is on the left. On the right are the building now occupied by IsaBell K. Horsley Real Estate; Richardson's; and the old Marchant Department Store, a wooden structure that stood where the Halcyon Building is today. The Horsley Real Estate building conveyed in 1923 from the Odd Fellows to W. Frank Hudgins, whose will referenced a cooling room, shed, and smokehouse on the property.

The first bankers in Mathews, L.E. Mumford and J.P. Nottingham, came from the Eastern Shore in the early 1900s. The Bank of Mathews, established in 1912, later merged with the Farmers' and Fishermen's Bank, which was directly across the street in what is now Hudgins Pharmacy. The Farmers Bank of Mathews operated from the building that now houses the public library until 1979.

This 1920s photograph of the east side of Main Street shows three familiar landmarks that grace the streetscape today: Sibley's General Store, which is now home to the Mathews County Visitor Information Center; the Bank of Mathews, now the Mathews Memorial Library; and Westville Disciples of Christ. To the left of the bank was Wolffe and Foster, also referred to as the Wyatt Wolffe store.

The building that currently houses Hudgins Pharmacy (also called Hudgins Drug) was originally the Farmers and Fishermens Bank, formed in 1920 by lawyer Joseph E. Healy. In 1928, C. Bernard Hudgins and his brother Bailey moved their drugstore and pharmacy here from a nearby location and shared space with the bank. The bank eventually moved across the street to form Farmers Bank of Mathews. Hudgins Pharmacy is still in business today.

Christie Chevrolet, at 330 Main Street in Mathews, was once home to Twigg Motor Company, a Chevrolet and Oldsmobile dealership established in 1921 by E. Pratt Twigg, who ran the operation with his son and grandson, Wallace B. Twigg and Wallace B. Twigg Jr. In 1977, E. Pratt Twigg was cited by Chevrolet for being one of only 84 dealerships nationwide with over 50 years of service. He was also a founding member of the Mathews Yacht Club.

This 1930 Chevrolet is flanked by employees of the Twigg Motor Company. Travel on land was not easy, particularly before roads were paved, and the sale or purchase of a car was big news. Mathews Court House boasted several auto dealerships around this time, all of which also sold gasoline. The last dealership to operate on Main Street, Christie Chevrolet, stopped selling automobiles in 2010.

This 1930s image shows the Court Green surrounded by a wooden fence and provides a glimpse of the familiar debtor's jail. The sign for the South Hotel is a reminder that hotels were once an integral part of the downtown scene. Some of them included the Davis Hotel, Virginia Hotel, Mathews Hotel, Marchant's, Sleet's, and South's. Today's view of the Court House square is described in its National Register nomination as a "handsome, well-integrated complex of buildings and monuments."

Completed in 1933, the building in the foreground on the Court Green was the original Mathews Memorial Library, funded in part by ice cream socials and art exhibits. The library, dedicated to World War I veterans, closed for a lengthy period of time after the hurricane of 1933 soaked most of the books. The library moved to the former Farmers Bank of Mathews building on Main Street, and today, the building is home to the offices of the Mathews County public schools.

Mathews Court House in the Early 20th Century

This 1935 image shows how close Put-In Creek, an arm of the East River, came to the Court Green before filling in. This body of water was originally called Puddin' (or Pudden) Creek because, as the story goes, a servant boy carrying pudding to a sick neighbor fell into the creek while crossing a narrow footbridge. The building that currently houses the White Dog Inn is also shown. Today, this area includes the Mathews Volunteer Fire Department and the water treatment plant.

The Court Green and back facade of the former Farmers and Fishermens Bank building remain relatively unchanged over the decades. The older image shows some wooden buildings (on the right) that were later wiped out by fire. The *Mathews Journal* headlines from the 1920s describe a Daughters of the American Revolution (DAR) oyster lunch, a Christmas community sing-along, and a 1927 shooting match taking place on the green. Today, the location is still a focal point for the community.

Perhaps one of the most noticeable changes to the streetscape of Mathews Court House over time has been the disappearance of gas pumps along Main Street. Several are shown here outside of Twigg Motor Company, which, in more recent years, was home to Christie Chevrolet. Another change is the replacement of wooden structures with brick, which was more fire resistant.

Opened in 1924, the Mathews Ice Company, located on Route 14 on the site where an apartment complex and the former Sal's Pizza now stand, claimed in an advertisement to produce 15 tons of "clear, pure ice daily" in addition to offering "a large stock of groceries, ice cream, beverages, tobacco and confections." The Greene family operated this and two other plants, one at Bayside Wharf and another at Cricket Hill.

CHAPTER 2

MATHEWS COURT HOUSE IN THE MID-20TH CENTURY

This 1950s image shows Powell Motors, a Chrysler Plymouth dealership and repair shop housed in the building that now stands between Mary's Beauty Shop and the Mathews Visitor and Information Center. Other businesses here have included Colonial Variety, Silco, Dollar General, and a consignment shop.

Although the west side of Main Street looks practically the same today, the east side has changed drastically over time. The earlier image shows a mostly tree-lined streetscape with only a few businesses. Today's view includes Westville Baptist Church, the relatively new Mathews Post Office, the Food Lion shopping center, Mary's Beauty Shop, and a consignment shop. Richardson's, a drugstore and fountain shop owned by the Richardson family from 1921 to 2001, is now a restaurant and apartments.

In 1936, R.A. Bertschy purchased the Westville Theater, located between the current Halcyon Building and Hudgins Pharmacy, from G.S. Marchant. Bertschy ran the theater until it was sold to W.M. Minter in 1949. A 1940 headline from the *Mathews Journal* references Bertschy appealing the loss of a blue law case. At the time, Sunday movies were opposed by some ministers.

The building that now houses the Mathews Memorial Library was formerly the Farmers Bank of Mathews, constructed in 1923. The building has been expanded and enhanced, and it now includes a children's library, a public conference center, computer stations, and state-of-the-art research technology. In 2005, the library earned the nation's highest honor for extraordinary public service provided by a library.

This 1940s photograph of Main Street facing southeast shows L.M. Callis and Son (left), which now houses the Bay School of the Arts. Leonard M. Callis founded his store in 1899 on Water Street and sold hardware, farm machinery, and groceries. In 1919, the store was moved to this location, and the original wooden building burned in 1934. Today, the Bay School, a community arts center, has a gallery, an art supply store, and classrooms offering art education and outreach programs.

With mannequins in the window, E.A. and W.C. Foster's Department Store was a full-service department store. A 1940s advertisement boasted a dry goods department on the main floor, an extensive men's department on the first floor, and a women's department on the second floor. Today's view from this same spot shows very little change in the streetscape. Foster's is now known as the Halcyon Building, home of the Mathews Film Society.

In the early 1930s, the Mathews Journal reported that A&P briefly operated a seafood plant on Gwynn's Island. The A&P grocery store, located on Main Street near the present-day Food Lion shopping center, was a major fixture in the downtown area for several decades. In later years, the A&P expanded and was joined by other businesses, including a Western Auto, a furniture store, and the Mathews Post Office.

This view of the east side of Main Street includes the Tatterson Brothers Department Store and Sibley's General Store. Owned by that family for nearly a century, Sibley's was operated by Cecil Sibley from 1945 to 1987. Tatterson's offered dry cleaning services as well as "the latest styles and fashions in ladies' clothing—everything you need from head to toe," according to an advertisement. Today, the space where Tatterson's stood is vacant. In the 1960s and 1970s, it was a Ben Franklin.

This image of the corner of Brickbat Road and Main Street shows Joe's Place (also known as Snooks', left) and French's Pool Hall (next to Hudgins Pharmacy). In 1950, the *Mathews Journal* reported the opening of Elsie's Restaurant in the rear of French's Pool Hall. Today, the building houses Real Goods, which specializes in local Virginia foods and products, and the Village Cleaners. Over the years, Joe's Place became Fleet's Restaurant and other dining establishments, including an Irish pub.

On the east side of Main Street, where Mary's Beauty Shop now stands, was H.K. Taylor Motors, built in the 1920s. Previously a partner with S.C. Hutson at the Mathews Garage, Taylor bought out Hutson's share after returning from World War I. Cars were originally shipped unassembled by train from Philadelphia to West Point. Later, they were shipped by steamer, reassembled, and driven to Mathews. The building was completely destroyed by a fire in 1968.

This view from the corner of Main and Church Streets facing northeast shows H.K. Taylor Motors and provides a glimpse of the original shopping center, built in 1958. Anchored by an A&P grocery store, there was also an appliance store, a Western Auto, and the Mathews Post Office. The A&P later became Barracks IGA. The entire shopping strip was demolished in 2001 to make way for the new center, which includes the county's first Chinese restaurant, Shun Xing.

In 1957, parking was a challenge in downtown Mathews, even though angle parking was allowed on both sides of the street. This photograph from the east side of Main Street shows Hudgins Drug and French's Pool Hall (now Real Goods). Farther down was Joe's Place (currently vacant), owned by Joseph A. Davis; the building now housing Chef Todd's Restaurant; Gayle Shawn Home Appliances (currently Country Casuals); and Twigg Motors (Christie Auto Care).

The Mathews Volunteer Fire Department's modest building on the corner of Church Street and Brickbat Road has evolved over time to a more modern facility. This photograph shows Put-In Creek prior to the construction of the sewage treatment plant. After several devastating fires in the 1920s, steps were taken in the 1930s to organize a fire department. However, adequate fire protection didn't become a reality until the 1940s.

Constructed in 1958, the County Office Building was a late addition to the historical Mathews Court Green. At one time, the building provided offices for the county clerk, the commissioner of the revenue, the county treasurer, the attorney for the commonwealth, the Virginia Cooperative Extension Service, and the county administrator. Most of these offices are now housed in the new court complex of Liberty Square.

CHAPTER

Mathews Court House in the Late 20th Century

Up until the 1950s, this building, located to the left of the Mathews Visitor and Information Center, was home to Powell Motors and a Phillips 66 station before the Colonial Variety Store moved in. As of this writing, the building, like several other pieces of prime real estate in the Court House, stands vacant.

The debtor's jail is said to be the oldest building on the historical Court Green. The small one-room building housed the county's welfare office until 1958. This 1975 image shows the Mathews County Sheriff's Department headquartered here. The sheriff's offices later moved to the building that currently houses the school board before moving to the recently constructed Liberty Square court complex.

Although much of this view from the corner of Church and Water Streets has remained identical over the years, one major change stands out. In 1975 a new, two-story, 7,680-square-foot steel building for the Mathews Volunteer Fire Department was dedicated. In an era when most firefighters are salaried employees, a team of dedicated volunteers operates Mathews County's fire and rescue squads.

On Brickbat Road near historic Tompkins Cottage stands the building that once housed Mathews Supply Company and, later, the Mathews Furniture Store. Constructed in the 1950s, the building was damaged by fire in 1982, renovated in the early 1990s, and over the years, it has served as a restaurant, bar, and pool hall. As of 2011, the building is vacant.

Southwind Pizza, located at 44 Church Street and owned by Ned and Dia Lawless, operated as the Lee Miles General Store from the 1920s through the 1970s. Lee Miles was in business in the Court House as early as 1910 and built a new store in 1922, the same year he sold his property on the corner of Church and Main Streets to Dr. Ellis Richardson, who opened Richardson's Drug Store.

The Golden Brooks Shop was a popular women's clothing store run for over 45 years by Golden Brooks. In 1912, after working for G.S. Marchant in the Court House, Brooks left for Baltimore and was trained by French designers. She returned to Mathews County and worked for E.A. and W. C. Foster on Main Street before opening her own store in 1940. More recently, the property was the office of Dr. Bobby Stewart, and it is available for lease today.

In recent years, businesses have struggled to prosper in the Court House area. As times changed, more residents began commuting to urban areas such as Newport News, Williamsburg, and even Richmond for employment as well as for shopping needs. Commercial growth in nearby Gloucester likely contributed to Main Street's decline. This 1970s image shows Main Street prior to revitalization efforts started in the 1990s. Today, places like Chef Todd's thrive in buildings that were not long ago in a state of disrepair.

In between Hudgins Pharmacy and the Halcyon Building (then Foster's Department Store) on Main Street were the offices of various local doctors, including Bowles, Ransone, and Reed, where ERA Bay and River Real Estate is located today. To the right, where Charlie's Barber and Anne's Beauty Shoppe were once located, is the Animal Care Society's Potpourri Shoppe and Inside Out Body Shop.

With the nearest shopping mall an hour's drive across the river, Foster's Department Store filled the need for clothing, shoes, and other essentials without having to go to town, as the trip to Newport News or Hampton was often described. A split staircase lead customers to the next floor, and an ornate, old-fashioned, manual cash register was used until the store closed in the 1980s. A consignment shop is currently located in the streetfront section of the building.

In 1986, the first parish house for Kingston Episcopal on Main Street was demolished to make way for a larger brick replacement. Built in 1956, the original structure housed the parish offices, Sunday school classrooms, and various community activities. Today, the larger brick building, at 6,500 square feet, includes a kitchen, library, chapel, and stage area with seating for 300 people.

Before the Food Lion shopping center was built in the early 2000s, an A&P anchored a shopping strip that also included a Western Auto, a furniture store, and the Mathews Post Office. The first Western Auto in Mathews County was opened in 1949 by Wilbur Clements of Gloucester. Carlton Blanchard, Charles Duncan, and Ernest Lemonds were subsequent owners. The store closed in 1994.

A clue to a previous life of the building that currently houses Dilly Dally Emporium is the Texaco star embedded in the brickwork at the top. George Philpotts, a Texaco distributor who also ran a crab-packing plant and steamboat wharf in Mobjack, built the Texaco station in the 1920s, but it closed during the Depression. The building has also been the site of a bowling alley, a Western Auto, and, as shown in this photograph, the Craftsman Shop.

Since the 1940s, the Faulkner name has been associated with appliance sales in Mathews Court House. In 1954, James A. Faulkner Sr. and Norton Hurd of Deltaville partnered to form Hurd's Appliances. Faulkner relocated to the Odd Fellows Lodge Hall on Main Street in 1970.

In 1998, Curtis Keith Faulkner Sr. renamed the business Faulkner and Son. Today, the business, which also includes a collection of vintage appliances, is run by Keith Faulkner Jr., who has worked there since 1976.

This 1977 photograph shows the old Mathews Hotel, which was located on a now-vacant lot on the west side of Main Street near Moughon's. A 1926 headline in the *Mathews Journal* reported, "Richardson plans big hotel." Clarke Richardson owned the hotel when it was torn down in 1998. Some of the wood and slate were reportedly salvaged by the demolition crew. Today, all that remains are the brick columns that once marked the driveway.

The local hardware and supply store known today as Moughons was originally Sutton and Kline, shown in this 1979 photograph. C.E. Kline and S.E. Sutton, representatives for Southern States Cooperative farm products, opened the shop in the 1940s after their feed and farm supply store, based from the Mathews Ice Company, burned down. For several decades, they sold feed, seed, farm equipment, tools and chemicals, appliances, and even baby chicks. Today, Moughons sells many of the same items.

The building that now comprises Moughons, Inc., was previously two separate buildings. This image shows Sutton and Kline operating from what now serves as the main entrance to Moughons. Abingdon Cleaners was in a separate building with its own Main Street entrance. In addition to the storefront structure, a large storage area for feed and seed is located in the back.

Before receiving the coat of gray paint that signifies its connection to Moughons, Inc., this building was the home of Bob's Used Cars, owned by Bob Lemmon in the 1960s and 1970s. Cars available for sale lined both sides of the building. Mathews resident Renee Callis recalls test-driving a Mercedes Benz here. Today, the building serves as an extension of Moughons, Inc., and helps advertise its products and services.

In the early 1900s, the Improved Order of Red Men had three Mathews tribes and 12 lodges. This particular lodge, located in Mathews Court House, was moved during the 2010 Mathews Market Days by Harc, LLC, of Mathews, which developed the Mathews Town Center. The lodge is now adjacent to Westville Baptist Church and will soon house condominiums for residents 55 and older.

At the intersection of Routes 198 and 14 entering the Court House, Hyco Corner looks very different today than it did in 1964, when Roland Wilson's Texaco station sold gas for 31¢ a gallon. Today, the county's first fast-food chain, Hardee's, sits at this busy intersection. The home in the background has been replaced by the new Town Center development, which includes a Dollar General, a Subway, an ABC (Alcoholic Beverage Control) store, and professional offices.

In 1969, the building that would become the Virginia ABC store was completed. Dr. W. Lennon, a dentist and developer, built this and several other structures, including Squire Supermarket, which is now Best Value. In the 2000s, the ABC store moved to the nearby Town Center development. Since then and after some minor renovations, the building has been home to the Medicine Shoppe and now the Mathews Pharmacy, offering the county's first and only drive-through prescription window.

The streetscape between Bank of America and the new court complex has changed dramatically in the past two decades. This 1988 photograph shows the Mathews Ice Company in a state of disrepair just prior to its demolition. The Mathews Dairies, which produced ice cream and butter, operated nearby. The building that until the late 2000s was Sal's Pizza is shown on the right. An apartment complex has taken the place of the ice plant.

This image shows one of the many iterations of Lee-Jackson Elementary School, which was originally a high school. Its unfortunate history of fires includes a 1922 blaze that burned a wooden structure to the ground. A subsequent 1932 fire meant more rebuilding. In the 2000s, the brick building was demolished to make way for the new county court complex, Liberty Square. Lee-Jackson is now collocated with Thomas Hunter Middle School on the property formerly known as Mathews Intermediate School.

This 1979 photograph shows the then-new offices of the Farmers Bank of Mathews. The sign associated with this bank was destined to change names several times over the next 20 years, as mergers with larger financial institutions became inevitable. In the 1980s, Farmers Bank was acquired by Sovran Bank, which was acquired by NationsBank in the 1990s. Today, it is a Bank of America.

The older part of what is now Lee-Jackson Elementary and Thomas Hunter Middle Schools was originally Thomas Hunter High School, a school for African Americans prior to total integration in 1969. J. Murray Brooks of Blakes was principal for 28 years. Prior to when the brick structure was completed in 1953, students had no gymnasium. Courses and extracurricular activities were extremely limited due to the small student population. Today, the much-improved facility includes a track and baseball and soccer fields.

COUNTRY STORES AND POST OFFICES

Like all general merchandise stores in the county, C.W. Downs and Son, located on Route 609 in Onemo, provided more than just the items that could not be raised or manufactured on the family farms. These stores, which often included the local post office, were sometimes the only source of information and communication with the outside world.

Tucked inside a sharp bend in the road where Route 198 meets Cobbs Creek Lane sits a building that was once E. Lumpkin Soles's Just a Country Store, which sold gasoline, hardware, meats, and notions. The store changed hands over the next several decades and was more commonly known as Cobbs Creek Market, run by Charles Hudgins, who, along with his wife, Betsy, also owned Port Haywood Market. Stanstrings Pizza is now located here.

COUNTRY STORES AND POST OFFICES

Established in December 1853, Cobbs Creek Post Office is the fourth oldest in the county. Previously located in this early 1900s building adjacent to what is now Stanstrings Pizza, the post office shared space with a barbershop and a millinery store. Postmasters included Anne Diggs in 1960; Anne's mother, Vernah B. Williams, in 1934; and Anne's grandfather in 1869. Today, Cobbs Creek Post Office is located in a building that formerly was Cobbs Creek Elementary School.

At the intersection of Routes 198 and 653 stands the building that once housed Moon Post Office and Country Store. Established in 1902 by Jefferson Callis, the post office was inundated with postmark requests on July 20, 1969, to commemorate the landing on the moon. Today, the post office is located in a newer facility slightly farther down the road. The original building is vacant.

COUNTRY STORES AND POST OFFICES

On Route 602 in New Point stands the structure that was once the I.P. Hudgins & Son store and the New Point Post Office. For many years Hubert Hudgins, son of I.P., ran the store, which sold everything from bulk candy and loose tea to deck shoes and crab pot wire. His son, H. Bland Hudgins, was a well-known Mathews physician. Although the store is now closed, the post office still operates from the site.

Located near the intersection of Route 613 and 614, the Beaverlett Post Office and Store, established in 1923, was supposed to have been called Beaverdam, after the neighboring community. Since a Beaverdam Post Office already existed in Hanover County, the Richmond postmaster chose the name Beaverlett. Other nearby businesses, some of whose structures are still standing, included a planing mill, a gristmill, and a wheelwright shop. The post office closed in the early 1990s.

COUNTRY STORES AND POST OFFICES

Bavon Post Office, built around 1920 and established by Norman Burroughs in 1935, was at the corner of Route 14 and 600 near the lighthouse. The store and post office served as a primary source of communication with the outside world and, at one time, had the community's only telephone. Burroughs's daughter, Marion Grey Trusch, served as a teacher in Mathews for approximately 30 years. Today, the cheerful beacon still shines for visitors coming to or from the lighthouse.

Peary Post Office, which operated for almost 76 years, served approximately 55 families in the 1980s. When daily transactions dwindled to only four or five, postal officials determined it would be more cost effective to close the post office. About half the customers opted for lockboxes located throughout the area. Today, the building still stands, and it has been used as a private residence. Most Peary residents now have a Port Haywood address.

COUNTRY STORES AND POST OFFICES

The original post office at Port Haywood, at the intersection of Routes 608 and 14, was run by Charles H. Hudgins starting in 1871. In 1989, several structures, including the W. Irving Hudgins store, once used by Ellis C. Richardson as a drugstore, were torn down to make way for the new brick facility. In 1871, the post office served over 200 families; in 1989, there were approximately 250.

In 1897, Charles C. Soles ran a store and a post office near the intersection of Routes 3 (Windsor Road) and 198. The store, originally northwest of here, was moved to this location by Soles. Mail service was transferred to Clyde Kemp's nearby business in 1922. Bailey Adams continued to run Soles's store until 1969. During the 1970s, the building housed a snack bar and pool hall. Today, SeaFlor Construction is here.

When Capt. Joe Trader tried naming his new post office Trader in 1901, he discovered one already existed by that name at Diggs Wharf. He then suggested a reverse spelling, and the name Redart was given to a community originally and informally known as Hunleytown. The post office and store were originally located in a structure very near the brick building shown in this 1990 image. Today, the building is vacant.

This former store and post office, at the intersection of Routes 14 and 600, served the community known as Shadow. The original post office, established in 1921, was located nearby and served approximately 150 residents until it burned in 1930. When the mercantile and postal business at this location dwindled in the 1970s, the post office moved to a smaller building nearby that could accommodate only two or three customers.

COUNTRY STORES AND POST OFFICES

CHAPTER 5

BEYOND MATHEWS
COURT HOUSE

Mathews County is rich in interesting and noteworthy sites that were once vitally important to the community; however, today, these sites hardly give clues to their vibrant past. This image of Sandbank Wharf shows the once-thriving oyster shucking and packinghouse.

Serving as the unofficial symbol of Mathews County, the New Point Comfort Lighthouse was completed in 1804 by Elzy Burroughs, who also constructed lighthouses at Old Point Comfort and Smith Point. Burroughs, the first keeper, also built the keeper's dwelling shown in this image. Soil erosion was a problem as far back as the 1830s, when the keeper required a boat to get to mainland at high tides. Today, numerous efforts are underway to preserve the lighthouse.

These New Point ladies, lounging against a car with 1941 plates, were standing on oyster shells that came from the shucking and packinghouse that once stood near Sandbank Wharf, seen in the background. Sandbank, located at the end of Route 609, was demolished in the August 1933 storm and rebuilt thereafter, a trend that would continue over the years. Today, there's hardly a trace of the once-bustling wharf. (Then image courtesy of Johnny Pugh.)

Another wharf that succumbed to storms is Bayside, built in 1912 in Bavon at the end of what is now Old Bayside Drive. Colonial Oil Company, Taylor and Hutson, and the Mathews Ice plant all had a presence at Bayside. In 1954, Hurricane Hazel washed away the pier and its structures. Today, a pavilion, owned by the Mathews Land Conservancy and available for rent marks the spot of the once-thriving trading port.

Callis Wharf, located at the end of Route 634 on Gwynn's Island, has been integral to Mathews County's seafood industry since the 1800s. Capt. William James Callis and his son Walter Eugene Callis built the wharf, which was also a stop on the steamboat lines through 1935. Although the seafood industry has declined significantly in the past 20 years, the wharf is still in use by watermen today. (Then image courtesy of Johnny Pugh.)

The Islander Motel and Restaurant and Narrows Marina, opened in 1969 by Mr. and Mrs. William Jenkins on 12 prime waterfront acres, was once the premier vacation destination for anyone visiting the Tidewater area. Complete with tennis courts, shuffleboard, playground, and swimming pool, the Islander was as popular with Mathews residents, who were allowed to purchase summer pool memberships, as with tourists. After 2003's Hurricane Isabel, the motel closed; however, the marina remains open to the public.

This is a one-of-a-kind photograph of Ward's Corner, where Route 14 from Gloucester meets Route 198 (Buckley Hall Road). Aside from the obvious errors in the road sign, this image provides a rare glimpse of Ward's Restaurant, which is on the right with the Coke sign. Ward's Restaurant, which later became Jordan's and then Payne's, burned in 1970. Today, road crews are working to improve the busy intersection.

Mathews Dairy Freeze, also known as Emory's, stood at the busy intersection of Routes 14 and 198, also known as Ward's Corner. Emory and Hilda Callis ran their short-order restaurant from 1957 until 1993. Generations of Mathews residents visited Emory's, as much for the social aspect as the food. The road between Emory's and Mathews Court House was the place to be seen on weekends. The building was razed in 2004. The intersection was modified and improved in 2011.

At the corner of Routes 223 and 198 in Hudgins next to Donk's Theater stands the site of the former Sutts Bar-B-Q. Over the years, this building has been home to a pottery studio, a bait and tackle shop, and more recently, Western Shore Heating and Cooling before the latter moved next to Hudgins Post Office. The building is currently unoccupied.

On Route 198 in Hudgins is the site that was once Bill Dixon's gas and service station. In operation from the 1950s to the 1980s, well before the concept of self-service gasoline pumps, Dixon checked oil, washed windows, and pumped gas for each customer. Today, the gas pumps are gone and the building has been extensively renovated. The name Dixon remains on the car repair business run from here, and Wroten Oil occupies the other part of the building.

Although Mathews County is not exactly synonymous with nightlife, one place guaranteed to be lively in its heyday was Club 14, located on Route 14 in North. Club 14, owned and operated by Alandus Ware into the 1990s, boasted a lighted disco floor. In the 2000s, the building was extensively renovated to accommodate Coco Loco, a Mexican restaurant, and later, Cheerleaders, a sports bar that closed in 2011.

Built in 1879 and remodeled in 1922, the Methodist Tabernacle, located on Route 611, is on the National Registry of Historic Places. Revivals, considered special occasions for Mathews families, were held for two weeks here every summer. Methodist evangelists, song leaders, and visiting family members traveled by horse and buggy, as well as by steamer, from Norfolk and Baltimore and stayed in the homes of local churchgoers. Today, the tabernacle is privately owned.

Originally a part of Mathews Baptist Church, First Baptist Church had 291 members in 1865. The land for the present site was purchased in 1867, and at the time, the church was called Second Baptist. The congregation quickly outgrew the original structure, and in 1885, the current building was erected. Over time, a total of seven churches branched out from First Baptist, including Antioch, Ebenezer, Emmaus, Zion, Wayland, and Providence, which stood near what is now Thomas Hunter Middle School.

www.arcadiapublishing.com

Discover books about the town where you grew up, the cities where your friends and families live, the town where your parents met, or even that retirement spot you've been dreaming about. Our Web site provides history lovers with exclusive deals, advanced notification about new titles, e-mail alerts of author events, and much more.

MADE IN THE

Arcadia Publishing, the leading local history publisher in the United States, is committed to making history accessible and meaningful through publishing books that celebrate and preserve the heritage of America's people and places. Consistent with our mission to preserve history on a local level, this book was printed in South Carolina on American-made paper and manufactured entirely in the United States.

This book carries the accredited Forest Stewardship Council (FSC) label and is printed on 100 percent FSC-certified paper. Products carrying the FSC label are independently certified to assure consumers that they come from forests that are managed to meet the social, economic, and ecological needs of present and future generations.

FSC
Mixed Sources
Product group from well-managed
forests and other controlled sources

Cert no. SW-COC-001530
www.fsc.org
© 1996 Forest Stewardship Council

Find *Your* Place in History.